<u>Healin</u>

The Journey of Healing in the Things We Think We Know

Written By:

Christina Marie Jowers- Pope

DEDICATION

This book is dedicated to ALL of my family and friends who endured hearing this vision since 2018 and now have the pleasure of seeing it manifested in print. Thank you for not doubting the vision and for your full support. Thank you to everyone whose paths have crossed mine along this journey, you each played a part in making the journey what it has been for me. And most of all I want to Thank GOD letting me live to see it all happen. May God add blessings to the readers and supporters of Healing in Heels.

Foreword –

Quieted. Receptive. Stretched. Transformed.
This is the spiritual path I followed upon reading *Healing in Heels*.
Minister Christina Pope has allowed God to breathe through her again.

This text, like God, invited me to do something I've never done: *TRULY* reflect on the issues, the heels, in my life. The words within **quieted** my mind as I found relevance and gained an understanding of the historical aspects of heels. The spiritual implications allowed me to be **receptive**, mindful of the hindrances that can cause me not to walk in all God would have of me. It **stretched** and repositioned my feet so that my pronation can bear the weight when standing as I walk in the totality of the things of God. Ultimately, it **transformed** me. The very breath that it breathes gave me fortitude to walk in Kingdom Authority and Regal Readiness all for God's Glory.

If you were looking for that something or are simply interested in your spirit being quieted, receptive, stretched, and changed, I invite you to turn the page. Turn the pages of this book and inhale. You'll no longer be the same when you exhale, in your healing.

-Dr. Dominique Prince

Contents

Come Take A Walk With Me...

It was New Year's Eve and like every other New Year's Eve I was sitting in church! Yes, church! I have attended what we call Watch Night Service ever since I was sixteen years old. For clarification and unity purposes, Watch Night Service is a service held to give God praise for bringing you through another year, to hear the word or message for the coming year, to bring the New Year in by honoring and reverencing God, and of course to "watch" the New Year roll in. As I was sitting there, the phrase "healing in heels" popped up in my mind. I immediately had a confused look on my face because I had never heard that phrase before and it had absolutely nothing to do with anything going on in the service. I brushed it off and then immediately the words women's conference popped up in my mind. It was then that the light bulb went off in my head and I connected the two phrases together. This "healing in heels thing" was supposed to be a women's conference! Great! I finally got it, I thought. My only question now was who was going to be doing this awesome conference and where do I get my tickets? It sounds like it is going to be a good one. At least those were my thoughts.

I was quickly enlightened by the fact that, first, it was not just a conference, but a conference based on a book, and second, that I was the person assigned to do this mind-blowing task. I instantly went into, "Wait! What! Me? mode. All of this was taking place like a movie in my mind, and I am sure that my facial expressions were a sight to behold for those who may have glanced in my direction as this epiphany was occurring. After the shock factor had given its harsh sting, I resolved to jot down the title Healing in Heels and a few other things just to help me remember this encounter and move on for now. One thing I knew was this was going to be BIG and there was going to be plenty of work ahead. None of which I could start while sitting in this service, so I marked the information and decided to start digging into it later.

The following day I grabbed my notebook and read the random thoughts I had jotted down during service that night. Instantly the thoughts and ideas rushed to my mind and started pouring out as I brainstormed the concept of Healing in Heels. My first thoughts were: I am a High Heeled Shoe lover! So, Healing in Heels kind of fits me because I not only have a large collection and variety of high heels, but I actually prefer them as everyday shoes. High heels are more comfortable to me than flats or sneakers. I started thinking, this whole idea may not be as bad as I thought after all. I mean what would be easier for me to deal with than a topic on something that I know and love greatly? Little did I know where this journey would take me. I resolved that if I was going to do this book/conference thing it was going to be done right! I started writing down things I wanted to research and ideas for the conference. I knew I had never done nor had a clue how to do either, but I am always up for a challenge, so I knew I could figure it out.

But where do I start? Well, the beginning usually works well so I started with the title itself, Healing in Heels. Just like the video began to play in my head the first time I heard this phrase, it began again. This time it was more focused and more direct. What if the very thing you think you know so much about you really do not know as well as you think you do, was the predominant theme? I knew right then the research was going to be interesting. I was excited to discover even more about the topic of heels to "add" to a collection of what I already knew. At least, so I thought.

Since I would be looking into what I thought I knew, I figured just to be safe I would dig a little deeper into the words heal and heel themselves. The two words are pronounced the same and even have similar spelling, but their meanings are very different. After researching, studying and prayer I came to the conclusion that healing is a necessary process that must take place in order to become healthy or sound AGAIN. Which means something occurred that took you from a healthy and/or sound place and you must undergo a process to return to that place. Now healing

takes place naturally and spiritually. I assure you we will dig much deeper into that down the road. The word Heel refers to the rear portion of a foot.
Medically speaking, the entire weight of your body is managed by your feet.

Feet are primarily responsible for your balance. A heeled shoe, for the purposes of this book, is considered any shoe that raises the heel of your foot in any way. However, as we are beginning to see, things may be different than they appear. We will also use the acronym God gave me for the word HEELs to refer to the spiritual aspect of this word. In reference to the spiritual side of HEELs, the letters are represented in the following manner; H-hindrances, Enemy, E-entraps, L-lives. As I was researching the definitions of the words God gave me for this acronym, I discovered they all had a variety of definitions and usages. A Hindrance is anything that tries or is to be used to delay, block, or deter you. The Enemy is the spiritual force whose one goal is to steal, kill, and destroy the plans of God. So for the purposes of this book I took that information and formulated the following definitions for our consideration throughout the book. Entrap -to be put in a position of no escape. Life/ lives referring to the purpose and promise God has for our very existence on the earth. So simple but the spiritual version of HEELs are hindrances the enemy tries to entrap our lives! As I learned more about the natural and spiritual sides of these two words it was obvious what steps would follow.

I would step into the depths and breath of the metaphor itself as well as its' relative significance to a book, conference, and ultimate women's movement. Why this title? Yes, it is catchy, but what did it mean? That question was quickly answered as well once I realized that this journey was going to take me down a road to healing in the very areas, I thought I knew and understood well. In this case, HEELS! I began to think back on many times when I thought I understood something and later discovered I was completely off. There were various bible characters who thought they had things figured out and turned out to have completely missed the mark as well. Errors in areas where I am confident can sometimes occur more easily than I thought and were more frequent than I would have liked to admit. So, the concept of healing in areas we think we know, like our "heels", was becoming more and more a need for me to look into. It was not just as a book or conference for others to enjoy. I needed this just as much if not more than the people I thought it might help. I needed to heal for real! To do that, I needed to take a good look in both my natural and my spiritual closet. I invite you to take this journey with me as I began to Heal in Heels.

Introduction

There is one thing that fascinates me beyond measure and that is investigating things we think we know. I have always had a curiosity about things everyone else just takes as truth with no questions or doubts. I question those ideas to the fullest. Not because I think they are wrong or false, but because I want more than a "because I say so" or "It just is" answer. If something was true, prove it. Oftentimes, that gets me in trouble because most people like to just have a sense of normality and to question that brings on insecurities and upsets their sense of stability in some ways. People, in general, have no issue accepting things under the premise that some things just are because they are. In a world of so much uncertainty, the idea of normal or a constant is highly valued and protected over truth. If the vast majority agree to anything then it is accepted as fact and is guarded to the highest level. This, in some ways, is completely understandable and even beneficial to a degree because it provides a sense of unity and security. The downside to what we think we know is that sometimes it is not the truth.

G.I Joe said it best, "Knowing is half the battle." Events, theologies, and even traditions in our lives that we think we know and understand but have not truly investigated or examined can cause us to repeat, perpetuate, and even create cycles that we may not be aware of. There is an icebreaker game that we played in a psychology class I took in college called Telephone. The game is played with multiple people. The first person is given a sentence or phrase and has to whisper it to the next person. They are not allowed to repeat it or give any gestures. That person has to then repeat what they believe they heard to the next person the same way. This continues until it gets to the last person. That person has to say what they heard out loud. Now that sounds really simple in theory, but in reality, very few groups are able to end up with the exact same statement that they began with. Now imagine a message, tradition, theory, habit, or behavior being passed down over hundreds of years across multiple generations, in various areas, with changing cultural norms. How different do you think the message would be from the original if it had to be recited or spoken out loud? Could you imagine the drastic distance between what we think we know and the truth of that knowledge? That very idea is what drives me to always look into what I think I know to find the truth.

There are many areas of my life that I thought I knew the truth and after digging deep into them discovered I completely misunderstood, was misinformed, only had a partial understanding of, or was just completely wrong about. Surprisingly, even with the very origin of the High Heeled shoe that I love so much, I soon discovered it had hidden secrets as well. Even more of a shock was the revelation that I had based entire portions of my life on flawed ideas. This led me to some very disturbing places personally. I started looking into my behaviors, habits, emotional reactions, standards, traditions, and even my thought process. If I could, after all of these years, miss such pertinent information about something as simple as high heels, what else have I missed?

I began unraveling concepts that even I was uncomfortable digging into. Whenever the famous question "Would you like to introduce yourself and then tell us a little about you?" arose, I always felt at ease because one thing I knew a lot about was ME! There was no easier topic than me. I know me better than I know anyone or anything else. So that question was always an easy one for me until I began this journey. I quickly realized in order to write a book about healing and heels I would actually have to start with where I was wounded and I become comfortable with unraveling the fabric of what I knew to be true in every area. I would have to face the areas in my life where I was broken. I would have to admit, like many of the heels I wore, there was some level of un-comfortability, despite my consistent choice to walk in them daily. I would have to take the band aid off some wounds and not only address the wounds themselves but go much deeper than that. I would have to investigate the who, what, when, where, how, and why of issues that were in need of healing. I knew that I would have to face some known areas of concern and likely discover some that were unknown.

I knew I would have to start by examining myself both naturally and spiritually. Honestly that seemed fairly easy as well. I knew I had some of the typical daddy issues to address and that was pretty much it for me. Like my heels, everyone knows that certain shoes cause discomfort but there are easy fixes for most of it. So, concerning the daddy issue, I had already done my long process of ignoring the issue. Then addressing the issue. And ultimately forgiving the issue. So, I was healed! I can just write about that and Tada, I will be done! It would be as simple as adding an insole to your shoe. At least that is what I initially thought. I could simply explain the process I went through to "healing" and there you have it half of the book would be done! Of course, as I am sure you have already realized, nothing in this process would be as I "thought" I knew it would be.

As I began to unpack my "only issue" I realized not only was it nowhere near my "only" issue but that I had issues I had not even known existed. I started unpacking traumas and hurts that I had not even credited to myself as REAL issues. I discovered I had a laundry list of things as plentiful as the number of heels in my closet that I needed to address. I had issues with self -worth, people pleasing, fear, and abandonment just to name a few. Discovering all of these issues only led me to more questions. How did I collect all of these unaddressed issues? Where did they come from? Why am I just now noticing them? What damage have they caused? And ultimately what am I going to do about them? I had many questions, but the one resounding fact was I had issues, and they were REAL! Not only were they real but they most certainly had to be seriously addressed in order for true healing to take place.

As I sat there in what felt like a sea of issues and emotions, I began to feel defeated. I had always thought of myself as a strong individual who knew herself and was able to conquer the world. It was the same confidence that influenced my powerful strut in my favorite pair of stilettos. Yet somehow, in that moment, I just felt like a scared and broken little girl whose world just came crashing down around her. My entire idea of who I was seemed to be an absolute facade. I felt as though I had been living in a fairytale with characters who were nothing like the parts they played in real life. Like the runway in my mind had just been revealed as only the hallway to the bathroom. How could all of these hurts and wounds have been hidden from me for so long? I had lived my life based on the so-called lesson I had learned over the course of my life.

Now to discover that many of those "lessons" were developed out of hurts that I never even realized existed and had such a heavy influence on present day life was simply too much to bear. The truth was just as naked before as the moment I took off my four-inch heels and rediscovered that I am only five foot four on a good day. I wanted to end this journey before it went any further. This whole idea of a book about healing, for the first time, became such a far-fetched thing to have me, out of all people, do. I was obviously not the right person for this task at all. I had more issues than The Daily News! Surely, I was completely unqualified to write anything, much less a book on healing. My issues were REAL. I needed to be reading books on healing for myself, not writing one. But as usual, what I thought I knew was not all there was to the story. Yes, I had REAL issues and yes, I would have to deal with them. But writing the book would not only force me to do so, but it would also heal me and millions of others in the process. So, I took a deep breath, collected myself, and stood up out of that sea of issues and emotions. I would write this book, and nothing would stop me, not even ME.

I remembered, in elementary school, learning how to write paragraphs, our teacher showed us the concept of the thought web. They may call it something different nowadays given that elementary school was quite some time ago for me. However, I am sure the concept still remains. You begin by drawing a circle in the middle of a piece of paper. In that circle, which is the body of the spider, you write the main topic. You then draw straight lines leading away from that circle for supporting information and subtopics. Those lines are the spider's legs and create the "web", hints the concept title of the thought web. I took each issue and began to construct my webs. What I began to discover is that there were some character traits I accredited to myself that I could not really say I knew or could pinpoint why or how they developed.

I have always thought I knew myself but as I began to unpack the very essence of my habits, behaviors, and even my thought processes, I discovered that much of what I wrote off as "just me" may not have anything to do with me at its source. I am and have always been talkative, outgoing, and independent. I am also very smart, even though that is something I struggle with declaring publicly. All of these characteristics are relatively good things. What I had not realized is that some of the reasoning behind these traits were not so glamorous. For example, after much digging, prayer, and honest confessions, my talkativeness, in part, due to my fear of silence. Silence forced me to be alone with all of my thoughts and that was scary! I had so many of them running through my head at any given moment that talking forced me to streamline them towards targeted areas. It was hard for me to sit quietly.

That was the ultimate punishment for me, and I honestly just attributed it to the fact that I just had a lot more than others did to say. I am and have always been talkative. That is just me! Or could it be that this is a behavior I developed to help me cope with an issue I never even knew existed? Could talking just be an accommodation I used to manage the pain of an issue? Of course, everything is not as deep and dramatic as that. But what I would come to learn is that there are often things, traits, habits, and behaviors that we have taken on that we may not be aware of the root from which they were formed and existed.

What are some things you have taken on that you may have just counted as a part of your identity? We must take a genuine self-examination of ourselves and start sorting out the areas in our lives that may hinder us from living and fulfilling our purpose. Michael Jackson sang a song that said "I am talking to the man in the mirror. I am asking him to change his ways". Simply put, I am just asking that you take a look in the mirror and really see what is there. No, it may not all be pretty, and yes, it may reveal some areas of concern. No, the process of healing may not happen overnight. And yes, it will cost you something to walk through it. But I can assure you it is well worth every bit of the experience to heal for real. I had to stop trying to accommodate, explain, and rationalize how and why things were the way they were in my life and get to the place of understanding so I could no longer be bound by them. The bible states in Hosea 4:6 King James Version, "My people are destroyed for lack of knowledge:". Understanding and knowledge of yourself and who God made you to be is the beginning of living out your purpose in life.

After discovering the root of my talkativeness, am I no longer talkative? I am absolutely still just as talkative! I am just learning to manage my thoughts and how to enjoy silence versus being terrified of it. I am learning that my busy head is part of how God is able to use me like he does. It allows me to process things in a way that is unique to me and also helps me problem solve. Not addressing the "why" of my talkativeness and simply accommodating the issue of fear was blocking me from using one of the very gifts God gave me.

What if the thing that scares you the most was the very thing you were placed on the earth to use but you allowed something to block it? Sometimes the only way to get rid of the monster under the bed is to shine light on it. I know that may sound cliché or belittling, but the truth is some things we can only overcome by not allowing them to remain hidden. Expose them so that they no longer have the ability to hinder us. It would be a shame to be a public success yet remain a private failure because we would not address the hidden things of ourselves.

Talking is by no means a national crisis that needs to be addressed worldwide in order for the purpose of God to be fulfilled. And yes, there are valid reasons for that. It is a very good trait to have if you desire to do anything publicly. Being able to speak at a high level is a great attribute to have in many areas, careers, and for various platforms. Some people come from an environment where communication was highly encouraged. Others are highly intellectual and have a wealth of information that they enjoy sharing with others. Some people, like me, just do not care about silence.

No matter if there is an explanation for the characteristic/behavior or not- self-evaluation should still take place. If you are confident that one plus one equals two then there should be no problem with digging deeper than just the explanation of common knowledge to prove that to be true. If the idea of digging deeper into any area of your life causes any form of hesitation that is usually an indicator that you should do further examination into the matter.

You cannot heal what you will not reveal! If you will not confess that you have an area of concern you cannot properly treat it, neither will it   be healed. Imagine entering a doctor's office and when asked "What brings you in today?", you say, "Nothing." What would you think the outcome of that visit would be? You cannot logically expect help for something you did not disclose was an issue, can you? In the same way you cannot simply expect things to go away or be resolved if you never admit they exist. But so often that is exactly what we do both in the natural and in the spiritual aspects of our lives. We avoid addressing problem areas and choose to believe that because we are not actively dealing with them that they are not still an issue. It is the concept of "out of sight, out of mind" at its highest level. Unfortunately, it is one of the biggest tricks of the enemy and it is highly effective.

For me, concerning my daddy issues, I had deduced to feel that I was healed because I was able to be cordial and polite with my biological father with little to moderate effort. The truth is my "daddy issue" was not just a minor situation. My biological father lived in the same town as my mother and I most of my life. In spite of out close proximity he still was not present for the majority of things in my life. To be so close yet so far away from a parental figure did not just create a "daddy issue". It opened the door to so many additional issues, like abandonment, trust, and anger. So just because I was no longer abundantly furious at the mere mention of his name anymore, I concluded that I must be healed from THAT issue. WRONG! I was simply one step further in the healing process. And yes, it is most definitely going to take a process that would eventually be my lifestyle. It takes time, effort, and sometimes even assistance to completely heal. If you break a bone, you do not expect the doctor to place the cast over it and then immediately break it off to reveal your now healed bone. We all know that a physical injury has to be acknowledged, treated, and then it can begin the process to heal. It is the same for our spiritual wounds. We must allow ourselves the freedom to heal.

Just as no two fingerprints are the same, no two healing processes are the same. We can have the same issue and yet take completely different routes to fulfill our healing process. There is no one size fits all method to healing. I am sharing my journey and my process in hopes that they can assist you on your journey. Feel free to use it as a guide to discover the best path for you to take to Heal in whatever

HEELs you may have. There is a saying "You couldn't walk a mile in my shoes!", and I honestly encourage you not to attempt to do so. What it takes for you to heal should never be compared or measured against anyone else. You are unique and like it or not so are your issues. The quickest way to get discouraged and want to give up on this journey called life is to compare yourself to anyone else. As I will share later in this book more in-depth, sometimes we place ourselves in hardship trying to take on what we find appealing in someone else. You cannot be beaten by anyone being you. No one can beat you being YOU! Likewise, you will fail every time attempting to be someone else.

Ultimately this book addresses the fact that we all have REAL issues that we need to gain a fuller understanding of in order to obtain our complete healing. God walked me through this process and compared my issues to the shoe I love most heels! For me, and so many others, it made understanding and going through the process easier. Healing in H.E.E.L.s is not simply a cute phrase or a catchy slogan, it is an entire process and a lifestyle that will change the course of your life if you allow it. Are you ready to heal in your H.E.E.L.s with me?

Chapter 1: The Strut is Real (The reality of it all)

"Always wear high heels. Yes, they give you power. You move differently, sit differently, and even speak differently." – Carine Roitfeld.

This famous quote was made by Carine Roitfeld, a former editor-in-chief of Vogue Paris. My, what a true statement to make about a shoe many women build their lives around. God revealed that there are some amazing similarities between our relationship with high heels and our spiritual journey. And although this statement seems to ring true in so many lives, the reality of this so-called powerful, life changing "heel" may come as a shock to you.

Just as there are a variety of heels and shoe Styles there are a variety of spiritual heels! In our spiritual lives HEELs Stand for H-hindrances the enemy uses to entrap our lives. Just like natural heels come in all different versions, colors, styles, and sizes spiritual heels take on different appearances and show up in many forms as well. There are some natural heels that are for everyday use.

Some only are used for special occasions. Some are for certain life events. Some we wear to feel a certain emotion such as sexy or confident or powerful! Just as we all have a go to Natural heel or shoe, we also have a similar spiritual heel as well. Every shoe designer has a specific recognizable branding and style! Whether it is the red bottom of a stiletto by Louis Vuitton, or the platform and Sparkle of Jessica Simpson. You can recognize a shoe's designer by its characteristics and branding. So, it is with our spiritual heels as well. There is but one designer and his recognizable style is to steal, kill, and destroy. He designs all sorts of heels for every situation, in every size, color and style you could ever imagine. His top sellers are the super high heels called Pride. He also has a platform version called deception. For those not into super high heels he has the Box heel of low self. That one is a big hit because it comes in a variety of styles. You have low self-esteem, low self-worth, low self-confidence oh, and the latest low self-image.

Now don't get it twisted, this designer has one of the largest markets out there. Everyone from presidents to the homeless has had a pair! Now, unlike Stacy Adams or Louis Vuitton's these heels do not sound quite as appealing; but after checking my closet I found that I, myself, have several pairs and wear them often! After the shock of this reality hit me, I began digging into this unhealthy heel issue I had. I went through my spiritual closet like a mad woman. I was determined to find and get rid of every one of these designer's heels in my closet. I immediately noticed those platform "daddy issue" heels I never wore because I realized they were much higher than they appeared and way more comfortable than the let on. Next to those were an older pair of "people pleaser' 2000s. Now those ended up getting me into some major trouble that ultimately brought me my first child. Stacked on top of those were in a beat up box I found a pair of low self-worth. I looked at this box with such disappointment in myself for having these. The closest was stack high and wide but as I started opening the boxes I realized a lot of things, one of which was: getting rid of these heels wasn't going to be as easy as I thought in my mind. I just knew once I recognized them, I could just throw them out! Easy, simple, no problem! Boy was I wrong!

The first pair I reached to get rid of were right there in the front. These heels were my in-famous, go-to heels in the popular low-self brand. I had them in the style of low self-worth. You may have this pair too. My pair looked and felt like this: I tried to continually prove I had value to those around me. I felt that I only had value when I was doing something others struggled to do or could not do. This heel gave me my "super power" and made me feel valuable. I would not just be replaceable or forgettable with this heel. People would ask me questions assuming I knew the answers and I would strive to prove them right. In my mind that's where they saw value in me. I was trying to find my value through other people's eyes because I couldn't see it on my own but with this heel I stood out! So, I wore this pair of heels to work, to church, around my family, and even with my friends. They were my "everyday heels". And boy where they wore out! But even worn out they received so many compliments that I ended up getting another pair by the same designer called Pride! Now, this pair wouldn't let me throw away that everyday heel and a few others I had gotten and tucked away in my closet. You see the problem was I had broken them in so well they had become my least uncomfortable pair. I had worn them so much that they had become part of my identity. People knew me for those heels, and it would be strange to see me without them. Right?

So, there I was sitting with open shoe boxes surrounding me just shaking my head. What have I done? When and where did I even get out of these heels? Why did I even get them? And how much has this cost me? And I have friends who have heels too!
What in the world am I going to do? I had no idea, but I knew one thing though, I was going to find a way to deal with this heel issue no matter what! I would find a way to start a boycott against this designer and put him out of business!

Carine Ratfield was quoted saying "always wear heels". Yes, they give you power. Yes, you move differently, sit differently and even speak differently." Those of us who have ever worn a pair of heels know this to carry some validity. Regardless, if your experience was good or bad whether you fell in love with them or about to never encounter them again. It can be agreed upon by most that heals change how you feel, are perceived, and how you carry yourself. So, this may surprise or impact you: t the heel was not originally designed for women. No ladies and gentlemen, they were designed for men. Wait! What? Yes, in spite of the fact that heels are a notorious part of women's fashion they were originally never designed for women! In my search to understand this Infamous you I found that the very first heel was actually recorded as being created for male Warriors. Yes, that's right the strongest, bravest, toughest men were the reason heels were developed.

Warriors in the 16th century wore horses with stirrups. The heel was added to the bottom of their shoes to keep their feet from sliding through the stirrups. Shocking, I know. So how did we go from brave warriors wearing heels to now in the 20th first century women wearing heels? That journey may surprise you as well.

Kings of the 16th century often chose to wear warrior gear in a more fashionable way than the actual functionality of the gear. It was the same with the heels. Kings chose to have their heels decorated for fashion to be worn as a show of masculinity and status. So not to be confused with mere warriors, their heels were to be higher and more decorative than warrior heels to ensure that their status would be easily distinguishable. Here is where we have the first conversion of the heel from functionality to fashion. However, the heel was still only to be worn by men. Over time the queens, not to be outdone, decided they needed to be able to wear heels as well.

As a result, a decorative pair of heels was designed for the queen not being higher than her king's. This is where the high heel got introduced into women's fashion. Naturally speaking the heel transformed from a functional warrior tool into a decorative fashionable item to be worn by women. I learned all of this primarily through researching various articles about the true history of high heels from BBC.co.uk, Londonrunway.co.uk and fastcompany.com

This certainly has its level of initial shock but ultimately made sense once I thought about it. I remembered seeing images of "pilgrims" in my history books that wore heels and curly white wigs and portraits of kings with their long robes, stockings and heels. And being an 80's baby there was the infamous artist formerly known as "Prince" who strutted quite well in heels. So, the idea of men wearing heels was not far-fetched once I thought about it. As I stated initially, this journey will cause you to delve into what you "think" you know.

What I thought I had learned and now "knew" was that heels were not originally designed for women, which I could easily accept after just a short amount of light research. What I did not anticipate was the next level God would walk me through. Let's just say the STRUT became really REAL!

It has been a known trend to take warrior attire and make it fashionable throughout the ages. Camouflage patterns and prints along with various boots have been customized and made into fashion statement pieces worn by the masses for decades. Where things got REAL for me was when God posed a question to me concerning the connection of what was being done in the natural form to how that same trend is also present in the spiritual aspect of our lives. The question was: "How often do we want to appear to be something without the sacrifice, duty, or responsibility attached to it?" It is okay to pause reading right here to catch your breath. I most certainly had to! It was easy to accept the concept of men converting the heel that was meant for warfare and functionality into fashion until you have to ask yourself: what have you converted?

Have you converted being confident into pridefulness? What about discerning into being judgmental? Or maybe it was intuitive into a "know-it-all"? Maybe it was something much less atrocious like being loving into being a people pleaser. Were you tenacious or a bully? It could be that your conversion was a little softer: cautious into being fearful; or possibly the tricky conversion from motivated to greedy. I may not have named your particular conversion, but I am sure you get the idea. Regardless of your specific conversion, we must realize the conversion from functionality to fashion took place with the heel that the enemy desires to convert. He tries to turn what God has given you spiritually into something that will ultimately hinder you in life.

One thing is for certain, no matter what version of heel you prefer to use as a fashion accessory- it is well agreed upon and scientifically proven that wearing heels hinders your natural strut. And so it is, when we convert spiritual gifts into worldly attributes that they were never designed for. Once I started digging into this revelation, it opened a new door in my healing journey. When I began to dig into my spiritual closet to see what versions (or rather conversions) of heels I had owned, armed with the revelation that each "heel" originated with a Godly purpose in its creation; it made me look at them differently. I was no longer mortified that I was such a horrible hoarder of these miserable perverted heels, (over exaggeration intended) but I was encouraged to simply find the original purpose and allow my newfound STRUT to BE REAL!

I was quickly making progress on this journey. I was really proud of myself! No, writing this book would not be the simple breeze I initially thought. Even with the "get your life together moments," I experienced were not so bad;

at least that is what I thought. I am sure you have learned by now, dealing with what you "think you know" is trickier than you may expect. I had begun searching out the Godly reasons for "My Heels" and was motivated to start my new Strut when it occurred to me that I never took a look at the conversion from a male shoe to a woman's fashion statement. Remember, the heel was initially a male shoe and was used to show status and masculinity. Now, I must warn you, this is about to get really touchy. Now would be a good time to pause and gather yourself. Once you read this you will not be able to walk in ignorance of this thought. If you are ready, feel free to continue reading.

The next major question God posed to me was: why did the Queen want to wear such a masculine status piece? Well, after some -research- the primary role of a king is to rule over a kingdom. This position is only given through birthright. A queen, however, is only a queen through marriage and usually only has power in the absence of the King or his inability to rule due to illness. She usually ceremonies but governing power is the duty of the King. So back to the question- why would the Queen want such a masculine status piece for herself? This took some more digging but after thinking from the spiritual aspect, I landed back to the source of why the enemy exists.

In the bible it tells of how Satan was thrown out of heaven.

He originally was an angel in heaven who was in the presence of the Most High God which in itself should seem great. To be in heaven would be great but he was not simply in heaven, he was an angel. The bible described him as beautiful. But like the Queen, what he had was not enough. Envious of God and the power He had caused him to not only be thrown out of heaven, along with those he had convinced to follow him, but it also caused him to receive an ultimate sentence of torment in hell. Now, I am not saying wearing heels will send you to hell, ABSOLUTELY NOT!

It was not the heel that was the problem for the Queen. It was what she perceived them to represent that enticed her. The queen wanted to wear the heel to represent her power. This led to the high heel over time being a fashion statement for women. It gave women the perception and feeling of power. Like the enemy, it was the power he perceived that lured him into wanting to be higher than God. Again, how often do we pursue and convert things from function to fashion, only wanting the appearance and representation of a thing without the responsibility, duty, and sacrifice that is attached to it? Since I was being honest with myself, I had to admit that the "daddy issue" was a thing for me, not because I did not have a "daddy figure" in my life.

I most certainly did! My mother married a great guy when I was about 18months old who took care of my as his own. As I grew older I realized not only did he loved me but he gave me the very thing I thought I was missing, a "real dad". He was not just a DNA contributor but he showed up for me. Usually late and most likely tucked off running his mouth, but he was visibly there. He is "My Daddy"! I love him to the moon and back. He has a significant place in my heart and has had a major effect on me becoming the person I am. Without him I would not be a part of such an amazing family whom I love dearly and am a proud member of. My issue came from others making it their business to point out how "My Daddy" , or step father as some would call him, was not my "Real (biological) Dad". They made sure to tell me how much I looked like my "Real Dad". Even would go so far as to make statements like "I just saw your daddy yesterday at xyz." Knowing that "my daddy" would never be there I would respond in his defense only to be told "No I mean your "Real Dad'. I am from a small town where everybody knows your name is more than just a notion. So, hearing this as a child made me feel that I must be missing something. If he was such a "great guy" and supposedly "my daddy" whom I loved wasn't a "Real" dad then why don't I have this "Real" dad everybody keeps talking to me about. I began to desire something that I already had, but because it did not look like what others thought it should, they made it their priority to inform me of what they thought I was missing. This caused me to envy those who had their "Real Dads" in their lives and to despise my situation. The truth was I was in a much better position than even those who wanted to point out my supposed lack.

However, at the time I could not see that. This pursuit of obtaining what I thought I needed would have been detrimental had I fully obtained it. Had my biological father actually raised me I would not be the woman I am today and I would not have experienced love in the way I did and still do from people who had no obligation to love me at all. Much like God, "my daddy" and his entire family took me in and loved me when I could not benefit them in the least way. To this day I am just as much a member of the family as any biological member and because of that I learned that love is a choice and it is given freely. Biology does not make someone love you, just like people pleasing, or gifts, or manipulation does not make someone love you. It is a choice and if no one else choses to love you know that GOD does and He wants you to love you as He does. He pursued us when we had nothing to offer Him. He sees value in us. The question you should ask yourself is what have you pursued, for whatever reason, that you truthfully would be better without instead of pursuing the love and life God has for you?

Your issue, like your favorite style of heel, may not look exactly like mine but there are some general characteristics that resonate across the board. To understand those, we must further dig into the history of heels and address the conversion of the heel over time. The changing of styling along the way has caused a change in the appearance of heels similar to how the effects of societal norms has caused a change in how we view our "h.e.e.ls". As I am sure you know, there are such a vast variety of "heels/h.e.e.ls." At this point, to list them would almost be impossible. So, for the purpose of this book we will focus on just a few styles: the stiletto heel, wedge heel, and kitten heel. I chose the stiletto for it is the iconic symbol of the high heel industry and spiritually it will represent what you would label as your main issue. The wedge is known for its deception because it has a wider base and is thought to be a manageable heel option. For those who enjoy the look and feel of a high heel but craved the sense of control this offers the illusion of a heel along with a false sense of stability when wearing it. The wedge, spiritually will represent the area you feel is an issue you manage well or at least think you do. And last but certainly not least the kitten heel. It comes with the least height of all the heels but it to can cause a world of harm. Because its heel is so low most feel that it may not even qualify to be considered a part of the heel category. But like its spiritual parallel although it may seem small it still has an impact and should not be left unexposed.

Let's begin with the in-famous stiletto heel. A stiletto heel naturally is one the most iconic styles. It usually features a high arch and a more pointed heel giving it a more statuesque appearance. Needless to say, it also is known for how it accentuates a woman's legs and causes her to have a lifted appearance giving an overall more powerful silhouette and strut. It has been worn by some of the most powerful and iconic women from every facet ranging from the white house to the penthouse, to the boardroom to the courtroom, to the nightclub, to the stage, and beyond. It is notably one of the most recognized versions of heels in the fashion world. So, what does that look like for you spiritually? You may never strut in a stiletto in your life y I am sure you have this style in your spiritual closet. Need help finding it?

One way to start your search would be to begin with the answer to this question, "what would you say is the one thing you need to change about your personality? What is the one characteristic that if you changed it everyone would notice? Once you begin looking in your closet with this in mind it should become a little easier to find. It was a little tricky for me to narrow it down to just one. However, after a little digging my answer was that I wish I did not care what other people thought or felt about me as much as I did. I was not consumed by others' thoughts of me, but I discovered it did matter to me a lot more than I wanted to admit.

There was an issue that occurred at work one day that God used to point out this particular heel of mine. I was rushing out to head to work and as usual I had a pair of flats. Any true high heel lover knows you should not drive in your heels. You risk damaging the heel itself because of the position it has to rest in while driving. I mean clearly the heel is no longer for functionality; and driving is certainly a functional task. Consequently, you must have a pair of flats and then once you arrive at your destination you can easily change into your heels. And so, it was with me and this situation except I somehow left my heels. I did not realize it until I was standing in our morning meeting and my general manager walked past me and stopped to stare with an extremely astonished look on his face. I, not realizing his amazement, said "What? " I was curious to hear his explanation for his expression. I thought to myself, "You know me well, so what could be so different today? After all, we had worked together for years at this point." He looks at me and says "Wow, you are short!".

Now my "go-to-heel", spiritually speaking. was "low self-worth" and his statement made it evident that these would be the hardest to deal with. Like the stiletto heel, it not only gave me height naturally but made me feel higher and more powerful, which to me equaled value. This was made even more apparent by the actions I took next. I immediately ran to the store next door and bought another pair of heels. I simply could not take people seeing "the truth" of who I was. Honestly, this is what makes this heel so iconic naturally and spiritually. Think about it, would the infamous picture of Marylyn Monroe in her wind-blown white dress be as breathtaking if she were wearing a pair of black flats?

We would not dare to skip over the wedge and block version of heels. These have become quite popular for those who prefer the "feeling of stability" incorporated into their heel. And I do mean "feeling of", because this can honestly be one of the more dangerous heels for that very reason. Just like our spiritual lives when we feel that we are stable the truth of our danger can be overlooked. The wedge and block heels are STILL HEELs! It is still elevated and can range anywhere from one to four inches, which is very similar to the stiletto heel height. The bible says in 1 Corinthians 10:12. "Wherefore let him that thinketh he standeth take heed lest he fall." King James Version (KJV). This heel would be the thing or issue that you are confident you have a good handle on. For me that heel was the "Daddy issue". I thought I had managed it well but truthfully; I was in a more dangerous situation with it because I thought I had it under control. The truth was left unattended and if I was not as intentional with it as I was with my version of the stiletto I could easily fall in this one as well. Again, your version may not look like mine, but I am sure you have this style as well.

And I would be remiss if I failed to mention the all too famous Kitten heel. It is a tricky one! Often minimized and brushed to the side, sometimes not even considered as part of the heel category. Any alteration to the way God designed and purposed for you is now a hindrance. God is the ultimate designer, and this is what makes it a part of the H.E.E.L category. The tricky thing about this heel for me was that it was so easy to brush off as not a big deal. As with everything else I was discovering, this one seemed minute in comparison; so did I really need to deal with it at all? ABSOLUTELY! Unlike the block and wedge heels I personally have more trouble walking in a kitten heel because it gives such an in between feeling. It is does not feel like a flat and it does not give the same feeling as other heels. I oftentimes do not know how to properly walk in it because it falls directly on the borderline of heels. This heel presents such a problem because it can easily be dismissed as not a heel at all. Spiritually, this would be the thing you do not do all the time or wear (display) often. It would be like telling those "Little white lies' or forging your spouse's signature on something they may have been ok with in the past, but you did not mention this time. Maybe it is fudging the time clock because you were running late, but it seems ok because you do a lot for the company off the clock that should compensate for this "slight" adjustment. Truth be told, we all have this one as well but often it is ignored because of the illusion of the true severity of it.

Most go to this heel option in areas where they can justify the "small" issue. It is as though because there is a good explanation and it does not appear to have a grave or overarching effect on things we can brush them under the rug and not even address it as an issue. This heel is usually purchased as an occasion heel or may have even been a "hand-me-down" from previous generation. The outcomes of this heel do not seem to be anywhere near as risky and therefore can often be dismissed. The truth of the matter is God is so concerned with us that He knows the number of hairs on out head at any given time in our lives. He would not leave even a kitten heel issue unaddressed. As we all know little things can turn into big things when left unattended. So we must deal with them all! Every HEEL must GO!

No matter which one of these you may have, I am sure given enough time and focus we each could find our version of all of these; and possibly more some that we need to address. No one can force you to delve into your closet and sort through your heels but you. There is work involved and it will require you to live out a journey of healing. What do you put on to compensate for your true feelings or insecurities? For example, I purchased those stilettos of pride because I cared too deeply about how others thought of me. Those in combination with my pair of low self-worth to give that false sense of confidence and acceptance made the perfect set. My pair of kitten heels were my talkative habits. It was not really a big issue and generally did not cause major harm to anyone but it was purchased with my fear credit card and was gaining interest daily. There were many more pairs in my closet as I am sure are in yours. Even though it may seem overwhelming I assure you, it sure is worth it to begin to deal with the things you think you know.

The purpose for taking the time to understand the history of the physical heel is for you to also see a real life spiritual parallel and open the door for you to begin to deal with what you can not necessarily see. I believe one of the reasons God presented this journey to me using the concept of heels is because He knew I would be able to understand and relate to the visual comparison and representation of a shoe. I, like many of you have a working knowledge of heels and could easily see the connection once it was revealed to me. It helps me be able to deal with things I cannot see when I have a tangible object that parallels in concepts. Ultimately, regardless of which heels you may have discovered one thing remains sure, the strut is real. Knowing the history helps our strut become a real journey and ultimately a lifestyle of healing.

Chapter 2: The Struggle is Real Too!
The discomforts of being in them.

"Some see the lifestyle and want it, yet they don't see the struggle that comes with it."- author unknown

I have come across a lot of "truths" on this free journey, but this quote is one that I can say is probably one of the dearests to me. A dear friend of mine gave a great illustration during a marriage counseling session that I believe pairs perfectly with this statement. He talked about the difference between a "snapshot" and a "movie". He referred to a "snapshot" as a single image of a frozen moment in time with no context or background, like a photo on a social media platform. Whereas a "movie" provides settings, storylines, context, and supporting characters that give depth and clarity. People see a very small portion of our lives, the "snapshot", and want THAT without ever knowing the depth of the full reality of our lives, the "movie", that it took to get it.

The Book of Genesis records the 1st examples of struggles with desiring and pursuing things based on the assumed benefits yet having very little knowledge of the long-term effects and true cost associated with obtaining them. The same holds true when it comes to heels and applies to both our natural heels and our spiritual H.E.E.Ls. People generally only see what you look like in your heels with very little understanding of the struggle, discomfort, and even damage that can be associated with them. Naturally, high heels are one of the leading causes of foot, hip, and back pain and can even cause physical changes as well (VeryWellHeatlth.com). Spiritually speaking H.E.E.Ls are the root cause of emotional and mental struggles and can even cause character flaws that can alter your spiritual walk. With the possibility of such negative outcomes, why would anyone ever want anything to do with a heel? Well, to answer that you would have to continue to dig into what you think you know. So, as they say in the videos, "Let's get into it!"

I am sure we can all agree that the struggle of heels in any form is REAL! But to completely understand that statement we must begin with the word "struggle" itself. According to the Oxford Dictionary, "struggle" is a verb that refers to making forceful or violent efforts to free oneself from restraint or constraint. Despite the apparent discomfort and restrictions that come with wearing heels, they remain incredibly popular. Some people attribute this to the perceived feeling of power, the enhancement of one's appearance, or the sheer response, which makes the pain and discomfort worth it. Some would even say beauty is pain! But by now, I am sure you know we are going to dig deeper than that.

The deeper truth lies within the very nature of human beings which goes back to Adam and Eve. For those who may not know: Adam was the name of the first human, and he was created by God. He named the animals and tended to the Garden of Eden. He was given a helpmate, also made by God, named Eve. They had free reign to do as they wished in the garden. All of their needs were met. No power bill, mortgage, or car payments for them to worry about, or stress over. They had only one rule, which was to not eat the fruit of the tree of knowledge of good and evil. Sounds simple enough, right? However, Adam and Eve chose to eat the fruit. We won't have time to debate who was wrong or at fault, but we will focus on the reason they struggled and ultimately failed to make an obviously better decision. That one decision caused all mankind to be cursed with the penalty of sin, which is death.

No, the struggle of high heels would have to be pretty extreme to end in death, but the reason for the struggle in our natural and spiritual heels are the same that Adam and Eve encountered. We, in our human nature, desire things that we believe will satisfy us, despite what the consequences may be. Rather it be the latest red bottom heel or a piece of Grandma 's favorite red velvet cake, we all have something pleasurable to us that we choose to indulge in despite the negative consequences or effects it may have on us. As a result, what we experience pertaining to our natural and spiritual heels is that though we know they are not the best decision, something inside of us wants to be satisfied by it, and so, we fight between what we know is good or better versus what our flesh desires. We make violent efforts to free ourselves from feeling the restraint of the better choice.

Well, no, Christina, I just like high heels. It's not a struggle for me. At least that's what I told myself. You may not feel this way about high heels, but I am sure you have something that compares to this analogy. I had no struggle, especially not with my heels. But dealing with what I thought I knew revealed some deeper truth. My desire to wear high heels was rooted and I wanted to feel pretty and seen. I walked with authority that I honestly did not feel I had without them. They gained me compliments that my low self-worth wanted to hear. As much as I love them eventually, they hurt my feet as well. I know this and usually have a pair of "better choice" flats with me to switch if and when needed. Now again, this is my testimony, it may not be yours. However, I am certain if you took some time and thought about it, you would find your version of this same type of struggle. The struggle is with yourself. It is not wrong to wear heels, because knowing and understanding the root of our natural choices can help reveal our tendency to make certain spiritual choices.

No matter what your thing may be, take time to analyze why you made the choice. My mama always said: "if you don't know why you are doing something you don't need to do it!" You may never share your findings with others, but if you know, then, at least you have understanding and can make an informed decision. There is no doubt that we all face struggles in our lives for various reasons. As for high heels, I want you to choose to wear them from a different perspective. I want you to choose to see your struggles with a new sense of clarity and operate from a place of power, not poverty.

I always wondered why Eve didn't choose to tell the devil to eat off the tree since he knew so much about it. Or decide to eat something else. Could it be that she felt like something was missing even though she had everything she needed? Eve may not have felt that way, but I certainly have. I am beautiful! Even writing took a lot for me because I still struggle to believe it no matter how many others tell me. I put on my heels; I "feel" beautiful. The funny thing is the statement you look so pretty, does not change with or without the heels. I just feel like it's true with heels on. My not believing I am beautiful just as I am operating from a poverty mindset. This concluded that I make decisions believing I don't have enough, or I have a place of lack.

However, after working through the struggle I had about heels I now wear them from a place of power. I am beautiful with or without them, and at any moment, I can take them off and it does not take away from me or my beauty. You can make decisions from that place of power. You have triumphed and have conquered that battle. Still, be aware it is a journey, and you have to remain vigilant and intentional to stay in your place of power because one negative comment or slight comparison to someone else or negative suggestive thought can cause you to slip. Stay mindful and stay powerful because the struggle is real.

In order to completely overcome my struggle both naturally and spiritually, we have to first acknowledge that there is an issue. We have to acknowledge that the things we think we know about ourselves may not be the whole truth. Some things we have credited to our character, and we say this is who we are, are not us at all. There may have been habits picked up during a particular situation or time in our lives as a defense mechanism. There may be a trait subconsciously learned from those in our environment. Maybe you use an aggressive "fussing" tone as a form of endearment because you grew up hearing that tone followed by the statement "If I didn't love you I wouldn't fuss at you! ". Subconsciously, you associated "fussing" with love. That is a learned environmental habit that can easily be translated negatively in other settings were that tone is seen as demeaning. Or it could be that our sense of reality was incorrect and therefore, we developed ways to manage a false reality. Let's take another look at the previous example concerning tone. It could be that the "fussing" tone actually scares and frightens you, so to avoid the idea that those who love you make you feel unsafe or afraid you create the false reality that they use this tone "because they love me". The actual truth could be that neither of these are true. They could simply be fussy people. They could have learned the behavior themselves. They to could have been afraid and created a false reality that they no longer recognize as false.

When going through your closet you have to take a moment and grab your flats. Ground yourself. Settle in the totality of truth. In this case there is a true definition of love found in 1 Corinthians chapter 13 verse 4-7 NLT which states, Love is patient and kind. Love is not jealous or boastful or proud 5 or rude. It does not demand its own way. It is not irritable, and it keeps no record of being wronged. 6 It does not rejoice about injustice but rejoices whenever the truth wins out. 7 Love never gives up, never loses faith, is always hopeful, and endures through every circumstance. When we grab our flats and are able to look at things from a grounded and balanced place we can truly see where our HEELS for what they are and recognize others as well. Either way, if we do not evaluate ourselves genuinely, we can have issues that hinder us from what God has planned for our lives. Just like with high heels, there are many ways to make them temporarily less uncomfortable. However, given enough time, the pain will rear its ugly head again and we will be forced to make a decision yet again.

The easiest thing to do is to accommodate the problem. With our natural heels, we can buy cushions, and insoles, and adjust to a different size. All of which will temporarily relieve some discomfort. In our spiritual lives, we can choose to find scripture to make us feel comfortable in our mess. We can chose to surround ourselves with friends, who too struggle and encourage us in our unhealthy stances. We could also avoid the truth altogether by staying away from those we know will tell us the truth, the whole truth, and nothing but the truth. This can sometimes be referred to as protecting our peace when in reality, it is avoiding accountability. No matter what we used to accommodate our struggle. The truth is- it is still a struggle. We cannot just continue in a "This is who I am" mindset. We cannot accommodate wrongs because we do not want to confront them. And we have to admit that, even though we may be able to find explanations, justifications, or even accommodations for our struggle, does it mean that our choice to continue in wrong is right?

First Corinthians chapter 10, verses 12 through 13 says "wherefore let him that think he stands take heed lest he falls, 13 there have no temptation taken you, but such as is common to man; but God is faithful, who will not suffer you to be tempted above that you are able; but will with the temptation also make a way to escape, that you may be able to bear it." Even the Bible acknowledges that there are struggles, but it also lets us know that we have to be not only mindful when we think we understand things, but that even when we are in a struggle and tempted, there is always a way of escape so we can manage it. No struggle has to overtake you be it walking in high-heeled shoes or a spiritual struggle. There is always a way to escape, but in order to do so, you must first acknowledge that there is more to what you think you know and be open to addressing it, dealing with it and avoid simply accommodating it.

Like our natural heels, there is discomfort in wearing them. But as the scripture said, there is always a way of escape-or in "Healing in Heels" language "a pair of flats" waiting. So, ask yourself what is your heel? Choose the better choice, grab your flats, and walk in power. Are you accommodating the discomfort you feel from wearing it, are you committed to suffering through it, and just feel a desire from the perception of lack in your life? Choose the better choice, grab your flats, and walk in power.

Oxford Dictionary Define struggle as a verb which means to make forceful or violent efforts to get free of restraint or constriction. Rather it be male or female no one would deny that heels are restrictive which brings into question their extreme popularity. With all of the research, data, and testimonies of the pains, stress and discomfort of heels why do millions of people purchases and wear them? Some would say the feeling of power, the empowerment or enhancement to one's appearance, or even the sheer response they gain makes the pain, discomfort, and even the cost all worth it. Alessia Cara said "Beauty is pain, and there is Beauty in EVERYTHING!" By now, I am sure you know we are going to go deeper into than that.

Be not deceive. This is a spiritual war, against who God created and designed for you to be. And although the analogy God gave me to assist with explaining, illustrating, and comparing the battle is heels, there is nothing fashionable or glamorous about the realness of this attack. I have to remind you of the spiritual heel designer, who is the enemy of God, Satan, himself. He does not play fair, give up easily, nor is he a pushover. So, walking in power may come with challenges which is another reason, the struggle is real!

The definition of struggle included some very key terms, like, sports, sport, violent, and restraint. In order to get free, you will have to break, tear down, and even dismantle some traditions, thought processes, viewpoints, and habits that you have become comfortable in. Just as we break in a new pair of shoes, so that the stiffness and the tension, causing a heightened level of discomfort can be alleviated. We also break in our spiritual heels. When God created us, his plan was good! However, the enemy presented us with a pretty decorated heel that was extremely uncomfortable, and we broke them in until we not only tolerated them, but we also became comfortable in them, and even grew to prefer some of them.

Now this may sound like a stretch, especially for those who can't or don't wear or even enjoy heels. But again, it may not be heels that do it for you, so just replace the heels with whatever your thing is. I assure you the concept is applicable in anyone's life. For me, they are heels. I will recall my very first natural pair. Yes, I remember them well. Easter Sunday, 1900 and blah, blah, blah. We don't need those details just to know it was a long while ago. They were patent leather, shiny, Mary Jane style. I was a big girl now that my Easter shoes had a small block heel maybe a half inch high. My Momma got them for me and dressed me up. She loved pretty dresses and hats for Easter. She put some thick stockings on me and did my hair up all pretty and took pictures of me. She was so proud of how I looked, and everyone told me how pretty I was. They marveled at my outfit and told me what a big girl I was with my pretty Easter shoes on.

You see, I only wore these shoes for special occasions, mainly church. These heels were not for everyday use. However, it was my first taste of what would later become my everyday preference. Now that I had this amazing experience of attention, compliments and noticeable elevation from baby to big girl, going back to everyday life without it wasn't easy. I wanted to wear those Mary Jane shoes, everywhere. I mean, who wouldn't? I walked really pretty, like a princess and people treated me like royalty. They held my hand and took special care that I didn't get dirty. I loved it and never wanted to stop. Did my mom know that was the foreshadowing of a being sown? Of course not! Had she known I would have never worn heels a day in my life! My mom did not care about criticism from those who tried to impose their traditions, or fashion sense on her or her children when it came to her girls. She was going to do the very best for my sisters, and that no matter what that looks like to others.

I wanted to dress up every day. The response was everything to me. Not that I was a raggedy Andy on a normal day. I was cute every day! People tell me that every day. My mom dressed me all the time and I had a great aunt who helped raise me because my mom worked night shifts. She was my first custom clothing designer. She handmade me dresses which I loved! She pressed and not just ironed my clothes and helped keep me cute daily, but these heels were different. They triggered something in me that (until this experience) I had no awareness of.

My first pair of heels were amazing because it gave me worth. For the first time I felt worthy of all the compliments, accolades, and attention I received. Don't get me wrong, as I stated earlier, I was always cute based on the cultural standards. My hair was beautiful, thick, long, and hand a soft texture. I was always dressed in adorable girly clothes, with my hair combed, and I was always extremely smart. I often heard, "You are smart, just like your mother." She believed in educating me herself. So, I want to be crystal clear, in no way was I lacking any value as a person. I just did not feel the value and validity of the other as I did in heels.

The issue for me was although I knew these things about myself I also heard contradictions and opposing thoughts that countered what I was being raised and taught to believe about myself. The door to my closet was cracked open by the enemy and it allowed the whispers of others to shout over the voice of those who actually loved and cared for me. That is thing about Satan he always uses what is true and tries to twist it into a lie without you ever really realizing what is happening. I believed I was pretty but not really that pretty which is just about not pretty. I knew I was smart but not a genius so just a little smart. I struggled with Grammar and could not lean my states and capitols so I was practically dumb. So the more people told me the truth about me the less I started to believe them. Kids at school picked at me for thinking outside of the box or for being a "goodie 2 shoe". Those comments screamed loud in my ear and drowned out the constant reinforcements of my family and others. But with these heels on, now that gave me some sort of "super power". Now not only were people saying I was beautiful but they were taking actions. It was no longer just words of affirmation but there were treatments attached that solidified the words. Finally their words and actions were louder than the lies in my head and it seemed to all be attached to these heels.

But that is just how the enemy wants it. In that moment I was pulled in to that spiritual department store. With so many heels to choose from it was becoming even clearer how I ended up with so many pairs. I realize now that it was never the heels that gave me power. I already had power. I was uniquely me. It never was about if I was pretty, smart, or any of the other characteristics I thought mattered. My true power came from GOD who was in me and the truth He said about me was the only truth. Sometimes we face areas in our lives were the lie speaks louder than the truth. In those times we have to remember to grab our flats and get grounded in what God says about us and our situations so that THE truth can drown out the lies that surround us. We have to remember that people only see us in our heels and not the pain that they cause us or the price they cost. Should you listen to the affirmations of others, yes. Should you affirm yourself, certainly. But never allow outside forces or outside influences overshadow or replace pulling from true and living source, God. In my experience comparison is the mass murder of peace and since God is the prince of peace to be without is like being without Him. One thing I gained in from digging into this particular space in my closet was that I can rely on what

God says about me over anything else because His word never changes and the ultimate action of sending His son to die on the cross for me out weighs ANYTHING the enemy could ever tell me.

Does that mean I am never deal with this heel? It most certainly does not. It just means I know how to handle it when I am faced with wearing. I have some shoes, like those Mary Jane's that were only for church. They would not be conducive in other settings, like school, or the footraces in the neighborhood, or riding my bike up and down the dirt road. But just there are various heels for various occasions there are various scriptures and techniques for dealing with each of them. The heel itself is never the root of the problem. It is only the indicator that there is a problem. And I certainly had many more to go through.

My everyday spiritual heals are low, self-worth. Which simply means, although my value never changes, I struggle and fight to continue to feel that I am worthy of the response to my value just as I am. I battle with the feeling of not quite enough. I tend to operate as though my natural value is lacking and therefore I must do something or add something to make up the difference. I tend to attempt to add value in the spaces I feel a lack. While trying to rid myself of this heel I discovered this poverty mindset of low self -worth had transcended throughout my closet. I noticed I did not value my time, finances, or even relationships as I should. This everyday heel was truly effecting my everyday life. I thought it was giving me power but in reality it was doing just what heels do, hinder and restrict me from flowing in the true Power of God that was already within me. It caused me to overcompensate for the person I already was. I was everything I needed to be without any additions but my center was effected by the heels.

I tried to prove I was smart by trying to solve everything. Well first off that is not smart to even attempt because it sets you up to fail. It is impossible to know everything. But just like with Eve in the Garden, the enemy tempted her with fruit from the tree of knowledge of good and evil. At some point in our lives we have all wanted to know the details of how things would turn out. That is the main reason people run to psychics and even profits. They want to know all things. As if by us knowing we had the power to change anything. I am not defending Eve but I can say I understand the desire to know it all or at least a large chuck of it. If given a test, I want to answer all the questions correctly and if I didn't, I felt dumb. Even if it is 99 out of 100 and everyone else scored 60 or below, I still felt inadequate for missing so many. Now be clear, I probably did not even study to obtain the 99, but I would be disappointed, nonetheless. This may sound trivial but I would ask you to open your spiritual closet and see what your everyday heel is. What is it that you do so effortlessly that is hindering you? Is it body image, people pleasing, aggression, self-sabotaging, overcompensating, pride, perfection?

You see the tricky thing about heels, both naturally and spiritually, goes back to the original, purpose and creation of them both. Naturally heels were designed for functionality, protection, stability, and warfare. Spiritually, the concept was the same. What God put in you was holds that same purpose. However the enemy perverted the original purpose and twisted its use, just like the king and queen did with the original design of the warrior heel. Causing unnecessary pain and discomfort that we are still experiencing today. My beauty and intelligence are gifts from God meant to be used for His glory, to help His people, and to build the body of Christ. Yet, the enemy caused me to pursue a counterfeit, self-made version of gifts I had already internally. In essence, devaluing the very nature of them.

That first pair of heels gave me a reason to believe that what others always said about me daily. Not realizing it was only valuable because it was already true. The struggle we face with heels is the inner battle between knowing and having confidence in God and his plan and purpose for us, and our desire to feel it. We often overlook how important to God we really are. If your heel is "insecurity", you may over pack or, over plan, or become a super saver. None of which are negative things. However, if you're doing them because inwardly you struggle with feeling safe and feel that the only way you will be safe is if you secure it yourself then that heel has hindered and restricted your trust in God. Do you believe that God is your protector and provider? If he doesn't provide and protect you not even your best series of backup plans could save you.

My prayer is that by exposing my shoe collection you would have the courage, tools, awareness, and encouragement to clean out your closet, too, so that we don't pass the same down to others and generations to come. The enemy customizes designer heels for us all. His only mission is to kill, steal and destroy the purpose of God in our lives. He typically does that by dressing things up and making them so desirable that we don't initially recognize the consequences and struggles that come with them. The struggle may be real but so is our Healing!

Chapter 3

You have to pay the COST to be the Boss

I am sure we have all heard the phrase, "You have to pay the cost to be the Boss". You may have even used the phrase yourself when referring to a situation where you have made an investment that you felt warranted you certain privileges, rights, or access. The concept of cost and value is something that we learn fairly early in life. No one is exempt from this concept of cost. However, since the book addresses what we think we know, we will leave no stone unturned.

The general definition of cost is simply an amount or value that must be given in order to buy or obtain something. Simply put, cost is what you have to give in order to get something in return. This concept applies to the natural as well as the spiritual world and covers everything! Nothing in this world is free and that goes for heels, both naturally and spiritually. Now you may think that this would seem elementary compared to what we have discussed thus far but I assure you the true cost of our heels will surprise you. Well, at least it shocked me. I have had more shoes than I care to count over the course of my life and probably more heels than I care to admit in that time as well.

Beginning this journey of healing, I had to sit with the natural and spiritual heels surrounding me. I began to wonder just how much this cost me. How much had I invested in this product? I began glancing around and started to add up the amount of money that was spent on the natural heels and realized really quickly that this figure would be much higher than I would like to admit or imagined. I sat there thinking of the millions of better ways I could have spent this money, how I could have saved and maybe even been rich by now had I made a different decision. I honestly just chose to stop counting because it became so embarrassing to think about how much money was sitting there in the form of a shoe which as we discuss had its own set of natural struggles attached to them. Furthermore, if the natural heels cost so much, I dreaded thinking about what the spiritual heels' price tag would look like. How much time had I invested? How many great memories did I give up gaining these spiritual heels? Whose life was affected by my purchases? What would have happened had I made the choice to invest differently spiritually? Where could I have been had I not paid the cost these spiritual heels required? There were so many questions to ponder.

Truth be told, and it most certainly will, I rarely spent a lot of money on my natural heels. On average forty bucks was about what I spent on each pair. I had a few that were more, but overall, I was not spending hundreds of dollars per pair. After all, I am a mother and have struggled most of my life financially just to make ends meet and prying just to make it. I considered myself a wise shopper even in the area of shoes. I generally bought them in the sale and looked for the best deals I could find to feed my love of heels. This thought made me feel a little better about myself knowing that at least I got them for a better price than normal. I began to rationalize my spiritual heels in the same manner. I mean God can redeem time, right? Yes, there may be some things that cost me spiritually but God is able to make all things work together for good so it may have cost me, but it wasn't as bad as I thought seeing as though I received a good deal on them. I mean if you saw my collection you would understand. I had some really amazing looking heels naturally and spiritually.

Naturally, my heels were always excellent compliments to my outfits and some even held the show on their own. Spiritually speaking my heels weren't very different. I looked confident, outgoing, independent, and strong. So yes, the heels cost but look at how good I looked in them, plus I got a "good deal" on them. So how bad could it really be? Little did I know that the "good deal" I thought

I was getting came with some hidden costs. Naturally and spiritually speaking, these heels came with more cost than just what was on the sticker or that was initially displayed. As the journey continued, I began to unravel the true cost of what I had invested in and the total effect it had on my entire life and the lives of those attached to me.

Obviously, if my favorite shoes had massive warnings labels or images of disaster on the box or even blood stains all over the shoe, I would not be attracted to them. Attraction is one way I rationalized buying another heel when I know I have several at home. I would tell myself, "Yes I may have heels already, but I don't have this pair, or this style, or this color already." It never fails that this one eye-catching shoe sucks me in just when I say I don't need another pair of shoes, yet I am in the shoe store. You would think if I knew I did not need another pair of shoes that I would not be in the shoe store. Per usual the discount program or rewards app I signed up for alerted me that there was a sale and that I would get an even better deal than the one advertised so I have to stop by and at least look even though I know I don't need another pair. Isn't it strange how we can know we don't need something yet go to the very place that it is located while telling ourselves we don't need another one? Is the way the enemy gets us to fall in love with what is to our detriment? He wants to make them so attractive and make the deal seem so good that you don't want to miss out on a "good deal". It is not different spiritually or naturally. The same concept goes for both sets of heels.

Think about your favorite shoe store and their marketing tactics. The store is bright and well lit, giving off an energetic and enjoyable feeling of happiness. It's clean and the shoes have displays that show them off. There is uplifting music playing in the background, and the employees greet you with a smile and are ready and willing to help you in any way. The atmosphere is set for you to enjoy the experience to help numb the effects of the cost. The nicer the shoe store, the more costly the shoe. Some stores go as far as to even serve champagne while you are about to put shoes on. They realize that the sheer ambience of a store could not do enough to get you to purchase the shoe so, they override your senses by intoxicating you. The enemy is no different. He sets the atmosphere and numbs your senses to the true cost of your purchase. He decorates his heels with compliments and illusions that life is better with his hindrance than without. He makes the initial experience exciting, and enjoyable. If he didn't, no one would ever be foolish enough to buy them. They only show you the pros not the cons, banking on the fact that even if you see the cons, you would be so consumed with the atmosphere, and the experience that you would override your senses and discernment and make the purchase anyway.

The funny thing is that it works. He has memberships that give you access to his buy one get one free sales. He has free shipping, and even runs commercials daily. "Christina, that seems a little far-fetched," you may say. Okay, well let's see. One of my spiritual heels was a pair of low self-worth. After I obtained it, I got a pair of low self-esteem with much less convincing. Obviously, if I could not see the true value of myself, my outlook on how I feel others viewed me would be low as well. They were of equal or lesser value. If you have ever done any type of shopping, I am sure you have heard that term. However, if you have not, let me explain. When using a buy one, get one discount the store charges you for the first pair, however, the second pair must be of equal or lesser value to be considered "free."

What does this mean naturally and spiritually? It means that if you get two pairs of shoes, using this deal, you will pay the cost for the most expensive one, and the upfront cost of the second would not be charged to you. However, what most do not consider is: nothing is ever "free "! Secondly, the cost of the more expensive shoe is often inflated to offset the actual cost of the second. So, in reality, there is no buy one get one free. The company wins all the way around. They now have not one but two of their items freely advertised in the public. In addition, they have gained an employee working for them with no salary attached. To top it off they actually paid the company to become an employee. Sounds crazy right? But when others see you in your heels naturally, and spiritually, it looks attractive. So, without the enemy even paying you, you become the biggest advertisement for him and his designs. Unfortunately, this is one job you will not get any benefits from. There are no benefits available to you, nor do you get a salary. You do get to continually shop with the enemy and your future purchase seems to come with less initial cost. Unfortunately, not only do you pay the cost, but you cause others to begin to shop with the designer as well. You even begin to buy heels and pass them on to those you love.

We knowingly pass our heels on to others we love. Often times it is in the form of family behaviors or traditions. Other times we pass our heels on to those close to use in an effort to provide a defense against experiences we have encountered. One pair of heels I received as "hand-me-downs" were the in the style "insecurity". This particular pair was given as a protective measure and came in the form of hyper-independence. I was never directly told to never let anyone help me but it was inferred with statements like, "Be careful who you let help you. Some people only help so they can talk about you later." This heel caused me to never feel secure in asking for or needing help. It caused me to not trust the good in people but to always assume I would be more secure if no one helped me rather than allow others in only to later be hurt by those same people. Everyone has a circle of people that they influence, sometimes knowingly, sometime unknowingly. Someone is always watching and is envious of the essence of you. And believe it or not those who are closest to us are usually the benefactors of the heels we possess.

One of Satan's most popular buy one, get one specials include the heel of depression, with its partner, condemnation. If this shows up in your closet, you are not alone! This designer is extremely cunning and crafty. He has been working on these methods since the earth began. So don't feel bad at all. Again, this is about healing, and what we think we know. Once the truth is exposed, and our senses are alert again we can do something about our future decisions. We can now go into our closets and recognize when we need to make adjustments. Spiritually speaking, the enemy has many of us advertising for him unknowingly. Here is your eye-opening experience to see your employment status and get rid of his products as well as terminate your employment effective immediately. Hindrances have attracted others to his designs. How may you ask? Well, let's take a look at a couple of pairs I purchased with my BOGO discount.

We can use a couple of my go to heels, my pair of low self-esteem and low self-worth as the example. From all outward appearances, no one would assume I have either one of these heels. I appear very outgoing, I behave very confidently, and even courageously. Many would say these two heels could not possibly be mine at all. They are generally attracted to my "aura" of confidence, and even aspire to have what I exude for themselves; and there is the free advertisement I mentioned earlier. This heel looks alluring to others and seek them out not fully understanding their effects. Due to this purchase, not only do I suffer, but others who are connected to me do as well. Low- self is the collection I wear most. Yours may be different, but we all have a pair somewhere and the effects are the same. We paid the cost of walking in <u>H</u>indrance, the <u>E</u>nemy used to <u>E</u>ntrap our <u>L</u>ives.

How do we quit working for this horrible employer? We start by confessing that we have worked for him and now know better! We pulled the wool off other people's eyes. We help kill the illusions about these heels' cost, and we help others begin to clean out their closets too. We take the blinders off. We destroy the pairs that we purchased, collected, gifted and passed down. It may sound like a daunting task, but it is the only way. We can only take this designer off the market with the one thing He cannot win against, and that is truth! Although this designer is cunning and makes things attractive and alluring he does have a fierce competitor. His name is Jesus. He is a great doctor that specializes in the healing and deliverance of this designer's product. We will talk about his role and great works in depth a little later. For now, the first step is to completely discover and understand what we think we know about this designer and his tactics.

Now, of course, terminating employment, and destroying his products that I had been associated with for so many years would be a lot easier said than done. Remember the only way we can win against the enemy is by using the whole truth. One obstacle we all have is that we do not readily tell our whole truth and nothing but the truth testimonies, especially concerning areas of struggle. For example, we have no problem, saying I used to be an alcoholic, but God delivered me. We may leave part of the details about how that came about or even that it wasn't the first, second, or third time he delivered to us. This is just the longest I stayed delivered, and therefore I can tell you this part, and not really expose the real cost of that heel or its designer tactics. Unfortunately, even though you obtain some level of breakthrough, you still would not have terminated your employment completely. You see until you can show and tell the whole truth, people are still under the illusion. Therefore, healing and deliverance cannot fully take place. It would be like going to a shoe store and the clerk at the register says you know everything in here was marked up right before we ran this BOGO sale. I am sure you would be a little shocked and may even hesitate to purchase as frequently but after you have shopped and selected two pairs of shoes, knowing the initial cost, it would be hard to convince you to drop both pairs and walk out never to shop there again. Would you be willing to reconcile that even with the inflated cost you still were getting a good deal making the product worth the cost? Most would choose the second option and consider it still a good deal in spite of knowing the additional information about inflation. You only showing the good parts of your story, although true, would have the same effect. Either way, start somewhere! If you are able to, and if you are led to share all, then, do so. If healing begins with you whispering your story, do so. If it begins with a sticky note during prayer confessing to God, you did it, then do that. You just need to start wherever you can and terminate your employment, effective immediately. Revelation chapter 12 verse 11 says: And they have defeated him by the blood of the Lamb and by their testimony. NLT

Whatever attraction you had rather it be the look, the style, the "good deal", or simply the love of the heel, take time to evaluate what they actually cost you and those around you. You do have to pay the cost to be the boss and sometimes that cost is to realize you have to get rid of what you invested so much into in order to start over fresh and begin a new and better path. As the Boss you have to not only manage how much you spend (cost) but you have to also manage what you invest in (value). Is what you are investing in going to reap a harvest or is the hidden cost just an additional liability to you and your "company"? As you continue on this journey of healing, sit down with your spiritual and natural closets and take inventory of your investments. Galatians chapter 6 verses 7 and 8 say; 7 Do not be deceived: God cannot be mocked. A man reaps what he sows. 8 Whoever sows to please their flesh, from the flesh will reap destruction; whoever sows to please the

Spirit, from the Spirit will reap eternal life. Make sure you evaluate the hidden cost.

Chapter 4 - Do you have that in a size 8?

Not many years ago I learned a valuable lesson through my love of heels. I have a friend of mine who loved heels as well and her collection was even more extravagant than mine. One Sunday she strolled down the center aisle of the church in the most amazing pair of shoes I had seen in quite some time. They were a size ten, clear pump with a nude tipped toe and a nude heel. The shoe was a four-inch stiletto heel. The simplicity of the shoe with the peep of nude color gave a versatile look with an elegant flare. With a shoe like this, I had to do what any shoe lover would and ask the infamous question. "Where did you get that shoe from? I need that in an 8!" As we shared our love of the heel, she explained that she got it from a local retail store in the city. I made up my mind at that moment that I would go there as soon as possible to grab me a pair but in the size that would fit me, an 8.

This particular retail store had several locations, and I began to search each one of them for that magical shoe, site by site until I finally found it. I was extremely excited to finally find the shoe I had been longing for over the past few months. I reached inside the box and immediately checked the size. I screamed "Yes!" The box clearly said size eight on it, but I always check the shoe itself. Just because the box says that it is an eight doesn't always mean the shoes inside the box are an actual size eight. Side note, sometimes the packaging can be deceiving! You can think you are getting something that should fit you but what actually is inside may not be what it was originally represented to be. Thankfully this was not the case! It was truly a size eight. I had found "my" heel. I immediately did my "happy shoe" dance as I pulled the shoe out to admire it before trying it on. I was so excited! I finally found what I had spent all this time searching for and it was everything I thought it would be.

I hurriedly slipped my shoes off in preparation to see this gorgeous shoe finally grace my foot. I began to try it on in sheer excitement. My joy quickly accelerated and my "shoe high" was climaxing as I began to slide my foot into this glamorous shoe. I was so "pumped", pun intended, only for the rollercoaster of emotions to begin its infamous death drop. Just as quickly as my heart rate leaped upon discovery of the shoe in my size, it deflated like a balloon popped with a pin at a kid's birthday party. The moment I tried it on my joy ride began to coming to a crashing halt. I could not understand it. The shoe was definitely a size eight, I made sure of it, but for some reason it fit more like a size seven. I could not believe after all of this effort that this was the conclusion of my shoe hunt so, I continued to stuff my foot into the shoe anyway! Yes you read that correctly. But there is more to the story.

I finally stuffed my entire foot into the shoe, thinking once I got it on it would loosen up, but at the same time knowing deep inside that it wouldn't. I was committed at this point, so I had to go all the way. I added insult to injury, pun intended, by forcing the other shoe on as well. I rationalized this bad decision by telling myself that maybe I was putting too much pressure on one side with just one shoe on. I needed to balance my weight out and that would possibly make it better. As you can see, I was on a downward spiral in my decision making all in pursuit of this admirable shoe I saw on my friend. Don't judge me for my poor decision making without recalling that you properly have done something similar, it just wasn't a shoe. If you are wondering, yes, I am giving you the "you know what I am talking about side eye and smirk combo"!

I stood there looking in the mirror, finally standing in what my friend seemingly wore with ease, in utter discomfort. Unfortunately, the throbbing of my foot still could not deter me from purchasing this gorgeous shoe. Yes, I still bought the shoe. I had made up my mind that I had invested too much to just "let it go"! I had finally found what I had been searching for and it was "close enough" to what I wanted so I would just have to find a way to "make this work".

Now if you were reading this and remembering the time you were so intrigued by something or even someone and admired what you saw to the point where you searched it out for yourself, you are on the right track. The same way I admired that heel-I came to realize I admired some other things and pursued them quite the same way. I would not say I am an envious person, but I have seen things that I inwardly turned into silent goals and desires. I have seen things that looked really great from a distance but when I finally got up close and tried it for myself, I saw it was not really a good fit for me. However, pride, ego, doubt, low self-esteem, and I am sure many others all held me bound to the idea that I had to accept what I found anyway. I am a good ole country girl, so I grew up hearing lessons in the form of sayings like, "You made your bed, now you got to lie in it!" That pretty much means that once you fix a situation up it's your responsibility and you have to deal with it. In essence, the elders were letting you know that you have to stick with the mess you made and that no one else was obligated to "lie in" or deal with your mess. "They would say, "Be careful what you ask for, you just might get it.". This was a warning to think about what you were seeking after and all of the effects that actually obtaining it could have on you and those around you. Lastly, one of my favorite life lesson sayings was, "Everything that glitters ain't gold!" This was a warning that just because something has similar characteristics does not indicate that it has the same value. You would think with all of this great wisdom floating in my mind I would have had enough sense to not buy this shoe knowing that it was not comfortable and was not a good fit for me. How often do we know better and against our better judgment we still choose the opposite of what is best for us?

I bought my shoes and continued to rationalize the purchase to myself as I drove home. I even forced myself to override my feelings of remorse with "joy". I placed quotations around the word joy because it was not real joy. The truth was I did not want to be upset at myself or embarrassed for going through with something that I knew was not going to work well for me. I could not tell my friend that I finally found the shoe that I had so vocally admitted I loved and wanted but did not get it. I mean it was my size and it was exactly what I said I was looking for. I would be crazy not to try to work with it. Where would I find something else that is as good as this? I was sure that with a few accommodations I could make it work. I just needed some time, and I could work on it and make it a perfect fit for me. Does any of that sound like something you have told yourself when trying to force something that just wasn't a good fit for you? Hear this, the shoe was still amazing. This particular pair just wasn't the best fit for me. How often have you not only tried on the "shoe" and then felt like you needed to invest even more of yourself to "balance" things out thinking that would make things better? Have you ever continued to "stuff yourself" into a situation you knew was not for you but because of all you invested, who you told your desire to, or even who you invited on the search with you, you chose to "make it work"? I know I have probably more time than I would like to admit. The shoe was simply being a shoe. I looked for it, it did not come looking for me. I tried it on and knew it did not fit well before I purchased it. Now I have to figure out how to make it the least uncomfortable so I can tolerate it long enough to look happy in it. Deep down, I was loving the look and hating the feel of the shoe.

I know you can think of a time or two when this same thing played out in your life, and it wasn't a shoe that was the issue. Maybe it was a friendship or a relationship, or maybe it was a job, or an accepted invite that was your "heel". Either way I hope the overall theme of the analogy was recognizable in some portion of your life. If so, the rest of the story will open up space for you to heal in your particular H.E.E.L.

So, after months of wearing these shoes and getting a ton of compliments my friend and I went on a trip together during which an amazing thing happened. We were going to be gone on an overnight trip and of course I packed lightly, and by "lightly", I mean over packed as usual. I had four pairs of shoes, not including my driving flats, about three pairs of pants, two dress options, a few blouses, and of course two pajama options. As I was putting together my suitcase I pulled out "those heels". I went back and forth in my mind about bringing them. Did I want the compliments and the spicy addition to my outfit options, or would I go with something more practical? We were going to a women's conference where there would definitely be lines, walking, waiting, jumping, and if you know me, shouting (the dance version, if you know you know). I ultimately determined that I was on a mission and had work to do. I decided, even though the heel was cute, I could not be "hindered" by that heel for this assignment. I had work to do and no space for anything to slow me down or distract me. *You do realize that is what HEELs do, right?* I am talking about spiritual and natural heels. Heels change how you walk, move, stand and react to things. However, this conference was too important for anything to be in my way. Funny, given the right situation even your HEELs will not be able to stop you from getting the blessing you know you need.

On our ride there, I told my friend about this packing victory I had in choosing not to bring the shoe that I admired on her. To my surprise she did not bring hers either. I began to probe a little deeper and "CONFESS" that even though I love the shoe it was not very comfortable and that I had been receiving so many compliments while standing in what was hurting me, that I really did not want to get rid of them. After all, they were so cute, and I did not think I would find anything else like it. To my surprise she begins to shake her head and laugh. I asked what was so funny. She said "I wish you would have asked me about those shoes before you bought them. I would have told you they were uncomfortable for me too." Because of the investment I had already made I started to make accommodation to help lessen the pain.

I have recently heard of numbing sprays designed to numb your foot so that you don't feel the pain of wearing heels, but I have never used it. Honestly, I had to do research once I heard there was even such a thing. It turns out that numbing spray blocks the nerves from receiving the pain signal. Spiritually, I can definitely think of times I must have used some numbing spray to continue in some of the mess I was in. I had become numb, and dysfunction was normal. I did not feel the pain or stress of it anymore. Truth is numbing spray may be able to stop you from feeling it, but the pain does not go away and neither do the effects of the situation. Just because you can't feel it does not mean it is not there. My accommodation method was to "break it in". Meaning you wear the heel more in order to force the shoe to change shapes to accommodate your foot. Needless to say this does not work so well in the natural or in the spiritual sense. I usually get blisters, sore feet, and bruises trying to force something that does not fit. The same is true spiritually. You will be the one injured trying to force situations that were not designed for you.

I looked at my friend and said, "So, Wait! WHAT?! You mean to tell me that I went and sought out what I thought was just a cute shoe but in reality, I sought out your pain because it looked good on you?" I thought I was getting a glamorous shoe, and I was actually getting PAIN! She went on to tell me that had she known I wanted them so badly she would have warned me about them. She would have advised me to at least get a size larger because of the tight fit. The funny thing was that all this time I invested in wanting a shoe that was causing her pain. The catch was we stood in what was hurting so well that it made the shoe even more desirable to others. Sometimes we not only stay in what hurts us, but we make it look so good that we avertedly entice others to join in the pain. We can also choose to stay in a HEEL because we assume that others in similar HEELs can handle it, so we should be able to as well. What we do not realize is that they too are suffering and *hindered* by that very HEEL and are just waiting for a way of escape.

Here is your space to get delivered. You do not have to remain in a situation just because you caused it, sought it out, manufactured it, or even asked for it! The moment you realize you made an error you can decide to choose your freedom over staying in the pain. Am I saying that you get away free with no consequences? Certainly not! There are consequences to everything but, if there are consequences to everything why do you have to stay to compound the consequences of the bad decision? If I am going to reap what I sow I would want the choice to sow some good ones to counteract them. I still purchased the shoes. The money was spent. The time I spent searching for it was gone. The pain my feet endured had been felt. The frustration of knowing what I thought would be great only to find out it wasn't great for me had occurred and diminished. Long story made short: *IT HAPPENED*! But I don't have to stay there. I don't have to wear the shoes again. I can try another size or another shoe altogether. Every day I reached for that shoe I made a decision to *stay* in what I knew was not good for me. What HEEL are you choosing to stay in knowing it is not a good fit for you?

It is true that everything that glitters is not gold but that does not mean stop looking at things that glitter. Just try it for yourself. *Test it.* Have others who are mature and wise check it out with you so that you do not miss any hidden indicators, you should be careful what you ask for and you should believe you will get it. *Investigate* if getting what you asked for is really a good thing for you.

Chapter 5: Oh, my aching feet!

At this point on the journey of healing in my H.E.E.L s I have learned many things about myself and am grateful that God led me on this path. I do, however, want to make a few things crystal clear.

One, the journey doesn't end here! There are many more HEELs I have yet to deal with. Secondly, the discovery and acknowledgement of my HEELs is only the beginning portion of the journey. Once you understand them and acknowledge that they have hindered your life you must take the next step. It's time to deal with the consequences and damage that the HEELs have caused. So, it's time to ask the age-old question, "Is there a doctor in the house?" Remember, over time the wearing of heels causes aching feet, back issues, knee issues, hip pains, and many other discomforts naturally speaking. Spiritually speaking HEEL s cause heartbreak, depression, anxiety, frustrations, anger, and numerous other personality and behavioral alterations. In both the natural and spiritual cases heels have an effect and just acknowledging that does not alleviate any of its consequences. You will need to consult your primary physician to develop a treatment plan to begin to heal your body.

After my closet experience of being surrounded by heels and my encounter with the flood of memories that brought me to this place I came to the conclusion that this journey was necessary for me to not continue this saga for the rest of adulthood. It was time to take action! So, I asked God, "What now?" I understand where I am naturally and spiritually concerning these heels I have and still do love so much, but how do I deal with it going forward? In true Healing in Heels fashion, He had me dig, yet again into what I thought I knew.

Having been pregnant and delivering five, yes five, children I have had my share of doctor's appointments. So, the process is something that I am quite familiar with. But if I had learned nothing else on this journey, I learned to be careful about what I think I know. So immediately, I began to look into healing, naturally as well as spiritually, and the role the healthcare providers play in both processes. Not to my surprise God revealed many new things about the healing process I thought I knew so well.

1 Corinthians chapter 15 verse 46 says, What comes first is the natural body, then the spiritual body comes later, I have chosen to stick with that template as well and discuss the natural side of healing and then the spiritual side. Naturally, after the delivery of my children the doctors would come in and check on the baby and I to assess our status after such a traumatic occurrence. Delivery is not only hard on the mother, but it is hard on the baby as well. Can I express to you that any trauma you endure never only affects you. Others are always affected by your experience. But childbirth is a little extreme in comparison to high heels- so let's just talk about my daughter's knee injury. She got this injury playing sports, not wearing heels but the experience is what God used to really blow my mind. At the point of the injury she went down and went down pretty

hard. There were tears and screams that flowed from her innermost parts. Part of the reaction was the pain itself but the other significance in part was realizing that the future she envisioned had been dramatically altered in the blink of an eye. I could relate to that feeling in moments when a decision I made came crashing down right in front of me, but it altered way more than a sports season for me. I made a choice to have sex for the first time that resulted in me being pregnant and becoming a mother my senior year of High School. I had been accepted into college and wanted to become an attorney but the moment I became a mother my future changed. I am forever grateful to be a mother but that choice changed the course of my life forever. Fortunately, for my daughter, once that moment of pain and loss passed, we now had to deal with the beginning of just her knee healing journey and nothing more traumatic. I called the doctor to set up the appointment to have her seen and this is where the revelations really started flowing.

I started by looking up facilities and providers who specialized in sports medicine. Spiritually speaking you must seek help for your specific situation. To be clear I am an advocate for God and Therapy! You need to make sure you are seeking help from specialized providers. Now if that is your pastor, therapist, counselor, wise friends or family, you decide. But make sure you are not seeking help from people who are sick themselves. Imagine going to the doctor for a knee injury and everyone in the office is limping around and complaining of knee pain. How confident would you be in trusting your care to them? Well, it looks the same spiritually speaking when you run to people who have not done the work to heal themselves in the same area you are trying to heal in. Yet so often we do just that. For my baby girl I wanted to make sure whoever was going to treat her was the best I could find. I suggest you do the same for your spiritual providers.

Once I had made my choice, I called the office to set up an appointment. The person on the other end of the call greeted me and asked how she could help. I began to explain that I wanted to set up an appointment because my daughter had injured herself. What happened next jumped out at me like never before. She began to ask me a series of questions that had nothing to do with an appointment date or time. She asked about where the injury was, when it happened, where it happened, what had we done to the affected area since the incident, and a number of other questions that had nothing to do with an appointment date or time. All of these questions came with no mention of a date or time for an appointment which was what I called for. It is very likely that the start to your healing may begin with discussing things you think have nothing to do with what you are trying to heal. Be confident of this, it is all a part of the journey. Then she asked another important question. One I am sure we have all heard before. "What type of insurance coverage do you have?" As my children would say, "It hit differently" this time though. I realized that the type of coverage I had would have a major effect on my child's care. The decisions I made long ago concerning the type of coverage I wanted for my family now were front and center. Not only did I want to make sure I had the best coverage available, but I wanted to make sure my children were covered as well. A very reputable carrier handless my natural coverage but Jesus Christ covers us spiritually!

I am proud to say that they both allow for excellent coverage, but they still require your copay. A copay is the contribution you make towards the cost of treatment or services. *Revelation moment: no matter what type of coverage you have or treatment you undergo, you must participate from the beginning and throughout the entire process.* After obtaining all of this information she finally set up an actual date and time for us to see the doctor. She gave detailed instructions on what to bring, where to go and when to arrive. Once in the actual office we went to the counter to check in only to be greeted the same way as on the phone but this time asking for proof of identification and coverage. In a world where identity has become such a conversation, there are some things that medically and spiritually speaking identify you. Medically, either you are a male or a female. How you feel, view yourself, and even portray yourself does not matter when it comes to the way you are treated. You are either treated as a male or a female. You are not treated based on what you feel you are. You are treated based on the reality of who you are. Likewise, in the spiritual realm. You are either a sinner or you are saved. You can present yourself as a saint but if you are a sinner inwardly you are a sinner no matter how you present yourself. If you believe in the gospel of Jesus Christ and his death and resurrection, confess your sins, repent, and invite Him to be your Lord and savior you are saved! It does not matter the wrong you have done in the past, nor how people attempt to label you. You are saved and will be treated as such!

After getting checked in and verifying our identity and coverage. We were then told to have a seat in the waiting room. *Can I pause to encourage those of you who may be in the waiting room stage?* All sorts of things can run through your mind about what the doctor's reports could be, how the outcome of this visit could potentially change your life, or even how much this process would cost you. I want you to know all of those things certainly went through my mind as I sat there with my daughter. What stood out to me the most was understanding I had to make sure my baby healed from this. She had much more life in front of her and I was going to make sure she came through this and lived it to the fullest. The life that was waiting on her was more important than any of the other thoughts in mind, and your motivation to heal has to be based on the same central thought. The rest of your life is more valuable than anything you will face in this healing process. So, pursue it with all you have. The nurse finally called our names, and we jumped up... well I jumped up. My daughter wiggled up and limped to the doorway where the nurse stood. But before she let us back, she looked at the file and asked, "Are you Olivia?" to which she said yes. And then she looked at me and asked, "Are you mom?" I replied, "Yes." Now my thoughts were, "I just did all of this when I checked in why are we doing this again?" However, who you are, your identity, matters! Sometimes you need to repeat who you are not only to others but to yourself. With all the noise of society, social media, your peers, your family, and even the your own thoughts running ramped in your mind reminding yourself of who you truly are and help keep you grounded.

We finally get back to the patient area and the nurse begins her assessment. She gets my daughter's weight, and checks her vital signs, asks her about age, family history, last menstrual cycle, and numerous other things that seemingly had nothing to do with our reason for visiting, which was her knee. I cannot dig into the family history portion too deep, but just know it is all a part of the journey. She enters all of the information into the computer, and we finally get into an actual room where she begins to ask about the injury we came to deal with. She begins the same exact questions the lady on the phone asked when we made the appointment. Honestly, I was slightly annoyed that we are answering the same questions over again, but maybe she just needed to verify the receptionist filled everything out correctly. Either way, I was sure we finally got those details together and could finally move on from talking about it to dealing with it. After all, that is why we are here to get past the injury not to keep talking about it. The truth is you will have to talk about your HEEL over and over again. Don't let that deter you from continuing on the journey. There is a method to what may seem like madness.

After all of the questions she finally says, "The doctor will be with you shortly". As you can assume their definition of short and mine were not the same. Here we were yet again in a waiting stage. It may be a very similar experience in your spiritual journey as well where you alternate between talking about the issues to waiting, from waiting to talking again, and then back to waiting. During this time, you can begin to feel like you are getting nowhere and that the journey is not benefiting you at all. But hold, the doctor, Jesus, is on the way, and He will come see about you. Then there was a knock on the door, and we heard a voice say, "Olivia?" She answered, "Yes!" Now I am super churchy and that alone is enough for me to take off running, but I need to tell you the conclusion of this whole matter. I will hold that praise until the end of this book. He entered the room! Whew, I am trying my best to hold it together, but I must say *when Jesus is in the room everything you need is in the room, and you WILL recover if you listen and obey.*

He began to go over all of the information the receptionist, the front desk clerk, and the nurse had gathered while assessing Olivia's knee. He moved it around and pressed on it while asking her "Does this hurt?" "Does it hurt when I do this?" He was seemingly inflicting more pain on her and putting pressure on the injured area to determine the totality of the effect the injury had on the entire body. Oftentimes we think that our HEEL only affected one precise area when in reality it caused more damage than the naked eye could see. This is why we need to seek help from qualified, specialized, experienced providers. They can assess the total situation not just what you describe as the issue. After his assessment of the injury, he then began to assess her. He asked about her daily habits, her daily activities, how she felt about the injury, if she wanted to continue playing the very sport that she was injured playing. He asked these things because it matters where your mindset is when creating a treatment plan. Olivia loves her sports and injury or not she was going to go back to the very thing that caused the injury. The one thing no provider, including Dr. Jesus, will attempt to do, is override your will. If you go to the doctor for treatment but are determined to continue to return to the same HEEL that injured you, it does not matter how effective healing would be if you decided you are not going to stay away! That is not an effective treatment plan because it will not benefit YOU! The goal of the provider and the treatment plan is to get YOU healed.

To heal means to become sound or healthy AGAIN. Meaning that you at one point were once healthy and something occurred that transitioned you from that health state. To heal requires you to put in work to return to that original healthy state. A treatment plan is a series of actions that are designed to lead you back to that healthy state. Part of the reason you have to continually answer the same questions over and over is because they are trying to assess your mindset as well as obtain the information. I realized the more

Olivia described the moment of the injury the less severe it became. The longer the distance from the initial injury the less horrific the description of it became. All that time in the waiting stage was adding more and more distance between her and the incident rendering it less impactful on her life. Yes, it still hurt, and it would require a lot of effort to get back to a healthy state, but time was already doing some of the healing and she began to realize the pain was lessening already. This gave us both hope that she can fully recover from this. May I encourage you that the questions, the waiting, the identifying, the verifying of coverage, the waiting some more, the pressing, it is all worth it and it is working for your good.

After all of this, the doctor determines that since she is going to go back to doing what it was that injured her, the best plan was to strengthen her body to endure what she would not let go of. That is a whole topic of discussion that is way too deep to deal with in this book! However, I will say that some treatments are designed to help you survive what you will not let go of even though letting go would be better for you. He elected for her to undergo physical therapy -not surgery. He said I could surgically repair the issue in about thirty minutes to an hour, but it would not be beneficial because as soon as she goes back to the sport, she would just tear the work apart and it would cause even more damage than it did this time. Sometimes, there is a quick fix to our healing but because we love what causes us pain more than we love being healthy we would create an even worse injury than we currently have. This would be due to our lack of respect for the repair that was done for our healing. So, Olivia had to go to physical therapy two times per week for six weeks enduring hours of pain in efforts to strengthen not only the injured area but the surrounding areas as well. When you are healing you need to strengthen the area that was injured and the areas around it if you want your efforts to have a lasting effect. Healing is a whole body, mind and soul journey. They are all intertwined and you cannot heal successfully without addressing them all.

Once the doctor had issued the orders for her treatment plan and explained how and why he prescribed the methods he did with her, he wrote at the bottom of the chart, "Once you complete the treatment plan, schedule a follow up visit.". It is not enough to simply just do the work to get better. You must go back for follow-up visits in order to make sure the treatment plan is working, as well as to see if any new habits or changes have created any new issues. Sometimes we focus our attention on an area so much that other areas begin to diminish due to the change in environment, usage, habits, or even mindset. Sometimes things get better across the board and treatments from previous plans are no longer needed due to habits created during the current plan. Olivia had to devote time at home to exercising her injured area. This caused a ripple effect: but because she was exercising it motivated the whole house to get moving more. That led to us eating a little healthier, and us checking our weight more. Just as much as your HEEL affects others, so does your HEALING. You are impactful. Your journey is worth it. It is important to not only you, but those you may not even realize you inspire.

Heels were made originally for warriors and rather you choose to wear them or not, you most certainly can take on the mindset of those the shoe was designed for and fight for your complete healing. Yes, the strut is real. Of course, you may have more to unpack than you thought. Yes, you have and will make some decisions that are not a good fit for you; and yes, it will affect those around you. Above all, as long as you commit to your healing journey, I assure you there is a Doctor who will be right there to care for your aching feet as you walk along the way and His name is Jesus. Whether you are addressing your natural heels or your spiritual HEELs make sure you remember that it is always ok to grab a pair of flats. Flats naturally are more comfortable and are shoes that offer grounded support and balance. Spiritually, that can be friends, family, counselors, therapist, pastors, or spiritual confidants. Whomever they may be, it is always ok to reach out to help you stabilize yourself, gain support and balance, as you continue on this journey of healing in the things you think you know.

Acknowledgements

I would like to first thank you for reading this book. I pray you not only enjoyed the read but were encouraged to delve into your own closets and investigate the things you think you know. I want to acknowledge everyone who assisted in the writing, editing, encouraging, and discovery of this book. You *all* are greatly appreciated and forever have my gratitude.

I honestly am not a good writer at all. My worst subject has always been English due to my grammar. That HEEL kept me from believing I could even write a book. BUT I DID IT! Flaws and all. I am grateful God gave me the courage to strut in the totality of ME.

I love you all. Continue to heal in

your heels and until the next book...

Strut on!

Made in the USA
Columbia, SC
28 April 2025

57259175R00054